THE **LIFE RECOVERY**

THE LIFE RECOVERY *Journal*®

*Becoming a New You—
One Step at a Time*

STEPHEN ARTERBURN
and DAVID STOOP

TYNDALE
MOMENTUM®

*The nonfiction imprint of
Tyndale House Publishers, Inc.*

Visit Tyndale online at www.tyndale.com.

TYNDALE, Tyndale's quill logo, and *Life Recovery* are registered trademarks of Tyndale House Publishers, Inc.

The brief excerpt from *Alcoholics Anonymous* and the Twelve Steps are reprinted and adapted with permission of Alcoholics Anonymous World Services, Inc. Permission to reprint and adapt the Twelve Steps does not mean that AAWS has reviewed or approved the contents of this publication, or that AAWS necessarily agrees with the views expressed herein. A.A. is a program of recovery from alcoholism *only*—use of the Twelve Steps in connection with programs and activities which are patterned after A.A., but which address other problems, or in any other non-A.A. context, does not imply otherwise. Additionally, while A.A. is a spiritual program, A.A. is not a religious program. Thus A. A. is not affiliated or allied with any sect, denomination, or specific religious belief.

The Life Recovery Journal: Becoming a New You—One Step at a Time

Designed by Timothy Botts

Edited by Susan Taylor

Scripture quotations are taken from the *Holy Bible*, New Living Translation, copyright © 1996, 2004, 2015 by Tyndale House Foundation. Used by permission of Tyndale House Publishers, Inc., Carol Stream, Illinois 60188. All rights reserved.

ISBN 978-1-4143-2823-2

Printed in the United States of America

24 23 22 21 20 19 18
13 12 11 10   9   8   7

CONTENTS

Twelve Steps

It's impossible to go through life without experiencing hurt. Even people who seem to have all the advantages (money, family, church background) end up with pain that no one can explain. We all respond differently to these hurts. Some of us turn to harmful behaviors or addictive substances—hoping to numb the pain within. Others try to distance themselves from it by throwing themselves into more noble pursuits—hoping to stay busy enough to silence painful memories from our past.

Over the years, millions of hurting people have found help and hope by working through the Twelve Steps of Alcoholics Anonymous. More recently, many who have not been addicted to alcohol or other addictive substances have also found healing through these steps. All of the Twelve Steps are rooted in spiritual principles that are displayed prominently in God's Word. *The Life Recovery Journal* has been designed for all of us whose lives have been touched in some way by addiction or compulsive behaviors. It is intended to help you make connections between the Twelve Steps, the truth of Scripture, and your own life. (Adapted from the Introduction to *The Twelve-Step Life Recovery Devotional.*)

Four Seasons: Heart, Soul, Mind, and Strength

As you work through this journal, it may be the first time you have gone through the Twelve Steps—but it probably won't be the last. As any person in recovery can tell you, the process is ongoing. It's not about racing through the Steps and crossing a finish line; recovery is a new way of living that requires reviewing and revisiting the Steps for a lifetime.

This journal is designed to guide you through the Twelve Steps four times in one year. The year is divided into four seasons, each one focused on a different image for the self: heart, soul, mind, and strength. These are the images Jesus used in Mark 12:29-30 to illustrate how we are to love God totally, with all of ourselves. As you work through the Twelve Steps in each area of your life, you'll reinforce what you're learning, and you'll gain insight into recovering as a whole person.

Two Tracks

Some people may prefer to concentrate on one step for a longer period of time. If you would rather do all the entries for each step before moving on to the next one, refer to the Index to the Twelve Steps on page 109 to find the next entry for the step you are working on.

Journaling Tips

- *Be honest.* All of the questions and quotes were selected to help you write open-ended, honest reflections. Don't worry about "getting the answer right." Your journaling will be boring, frustrating, and unhelpful if you're trying to write what someone else expects you to write.

- *Keep writing.* The questions and quotes in the journal should help you keep writing if you get stuck. But if you're still stuck and would rather write about something else entirely, go ahead! Just keep up the habit of writing.

- *Don't isolate yourself.* The questions in this journal are the sorts of questions a counselor or a sponsor might ask—but they're no replacement for a real sponsor! It's a good idea to share what you've been writing with your sponsor and get feedback. He or she may see something about you that you can't see in yourself.

SEASON 1
HEART

Recovery begins with a change of heart. Other people may try to convince us that we have a problem. Inwardly, we may even agree that our lives are unmanageable and that we need to change. But recovery cannot begin until we desire it with our hearts, with the core of our wills. For many of us, that change of heart happens only after we've hit rock bottom.

Even after we experience the change of heart that starts us out on the road to recovery, we still desire many different, incompatible things. We want recovery, yes, but we also want to maintain our dignity, the appearance of being in control, our independence, and our familiar habits. On some level, we even want to hold on to the addictions that have made our lives unmanageable.

As you work the Twelve Steps in this first season, you will be challenged to redirect your heart to desire what is right. As your heart changes its direction, the rest of your life will follow.

WEEK 1

STEP ONE: We admitted that we were powerless over our problems and that our lives had become unmanageable.

"Life doesn't always follow our rules or any other set of rules that might help us predict how things will happen. Even the truth of the Bible leaves room for a struggle between the forces of good and evil. There are times when we do our best, try our hardest to be good, and apply ourselves completely. But life still doesn't work out the way we think it should" (from Step One, Day 29 of *The Life Recovery Devotional*).

Right now, what isn't working out the way I think it should? How is it different from what I expected? What are some things that could account for the differences?

My marriage - the intimacy part of it. While I see awesome fruit in my overall marital intimacy, the sexual part seems so "stuck." Trauma to Christie (lots caused by me) plays a big role.

Scripture

I don't really understand myself, for I want to do what is right, but I don't do it. Instead, I do what I hate. But if I know that what I am doing is wrong, this shows that I agree that the law is good. So I am not the one doing wrong; it is sin living in me that does it. And I know that nothing good lives in me, that is, in my sinful nature. I want to do what is right, but I can't. I want to do what is good, but I don't. I don't want to do what is wrong, but I do it anyway. But if I do what I don't want to do, I am not really the one doing wrong; it is sin living in me that does it.
ROMANS 7:15-20

Does this passage from Romans 7 resonate with me? When have I been frustrated by being unable to accomplish what I had meant to do? What prevented me from doing so?

Yes; So often in my struggle with lust I find myself doing what I hate. "Giving in" seems to be the default path often.

For Reflection

When in the past did I feel that I was not in control? What did I do to try to regain control? How did it turn out?

_____

_____

_____

Consider how the idea of "control" affects these relationships:

- my parents
- my spouse or significant other
- my son or daughter
- my brother or sister
- my boss
- a coworker
- a teacher
- another authority figure

Prayer

Pray through Psalm 116.

God, I admit that I am powerless, but you are powerful. I am limited, but you are sovereign. I am weak, but you are strong. I am in need, but you are complete. I am unfinished, but you are working in me.

God, I admit that I am out of control, but you are in control. I cannot manage, but you do all things well. I am looking for a way out, but you are looking for a way in.

God, I admit that I depend on myself, but you are more dependable. I depend on relationships, but you are more dependable. I depend on addictions and compulsions, but you are more dependable.

WEEK 2

STEP TWO: We came to believe that a Power greater than ourselves could restore us to sanity.

How has life been unfair to me (e.g., in the areas of family, trauma, addiction)? How does this affect my trust in a God who allowed these things to happen?

_____

_____

_____

Scripture
Come to me with your ears wide open. Listen, and you will find life. I will make an everlasting covenant with you. I will give you all the unfailing love I promised to David. See how I used him to display my power among the peoples. I made him a leader among the nations. . . . "My thoughts are nothing like your thoughts," says the LORD. "And my ways are far beyond anything you could imagine. For just as the heavens are higher

than the earth, so my ways are higher than your ways and my thoughts higher than your thoughts."
ISAIAH 55:3-4, 8-9

How might God be using my experiences to display his power "among the peoples"?

_____

_____

_____

All glory to God, who is able, through his mighty power at work within us, to accomplish infinitely more than we might ask or think.
EPHESIANS 3:20

For Reflection
If my restoration is not only for my good but also for God's glory, how does that motivate me? What does it motivate me to do?

_____

_____

_____

Prayer
Pray through Psalm 130, making it personal for where you are in life.

WEEK 3

STEP THREE: We made a decision to turn our wills and our lives over to the care of God.

I use my will to make decisions. What considerations did I take into account before making the decision to turn my life over to God? (Was that different from the way I normally make decisions?) How could I use that method for other decisions?

_____

_____

_____

Scripture
This is what the LORD says: "Cursed are those who put their trust in mere humans, who rely on human strength and turn their hearts away from the LORD. They are like stunted shrubs in the desert, with no hope for the future. They will live in the barren wilderness, in an uninhabited salty land. But blessed are those who trust in the LORD and have made the LORD their hope and confidence. They are like trees planted along a riverbank, with roots that reach deep into the water. Such trees are not bothered by the heat or worried by long months of drought. Their leaves stay green, and they never stop producing fruit. The human heart is the most deceitful of all things, and desperately wicked. Who really knows how bad it is? But I, the LORD, search all hearts and examine secret motives. I give all people their due rewards, according to what their actions deserve."
JEREMIAH 17:5-10

Where have I put my trust in the past? How does this decision in Step Three affect where I place my trust?

For Reflection

Trust almost always involves risk. What is there in me that I do not trust? What does it take for me to trust others? What will I have to let go of in order to trust God?

_____

_____

_____

_____

> *Give all your worries and cares to God,*
> *for he cares about you.*
> 1 PETER 5:7
>
> **What is one thing I am worrying**
> **about right now? How can I begin**
> **entrusting it to God's care?**

Prayer

Use Psalm 25 to focus your prayer. Allow it to guide your thoughts about yourself and about God.

WEEK 4

STEP FOUR: We made a searching and fearless moral inventory of ourselves.

What are the different spheres of relationship in my life? What does my moral inventory over the last few days look like for each sphere?

_____

_____

_____

_____

_____

Possible spheres:

- work
- home
- friends
- family
- church
- school

Scripture

The word of God is alive and powerful. It is sharper than the sharpest two-edged sword, cutting between soul and spirit, between joint and marrow. It exposes our innermost thoughts and desires. Nothing in all creation is hidden from God. Everything is naked and exposed before his eyes, and he is the one to whom we are accountable.

HEBREWS 4:12-13

What insights has God's Word given me as I take moral inventory?

_____

_____

_____

For Reflection

Fears can help me identify the big issues I'm facing. In what spheres of my life am I afraid to take inventory? With whom can I talk about my fears? Who can help me explore the reasons for them?

_____

_____

_____

Read 1 John 4:17-18 and Step Four,
Day 8 in *The Life Recovery Devotional*.

Prayer

Lord, these are the fears that I'm facing: _____
_____. I offer them to you. Give me the strength to face each one and wisdom to decide how to resolve each one. Grant me peace and clarity as I wrestle with each of these fears. Amen.

WEEK 5

STEP FIVE: We admitted to God, to ourselves, and to another human being the exact nature of our wrongs.

Admitting our faults and failures takes courage and humility. We face the possibility that once we have done so, those we care about will no longer accept us. In what relationships am I most worried about this?

_____

_____

_____

Scripture

Two people are better off than one, for they can help each other succeed. If one person falls, the other can reach out and help. But someone who falls alone is in real trouble. Likewise, two people lying close together can keep each other warm. But how can one be warm alone? A person standing alone can be attacked and defeated, but two can stand back-to-back and conquer. Three are even better, for a triple-braided cord is not easily broken. ECCLESIASTES 4:9-12

All relationships have conflict, but they can also be great sources of strength and encouragement. What conflicts am I facing right now? How can I strengthen and encourage those with whom I'm in conflict?

_____

_____

_____

For Reflection

I have chosen to admit my failures to another human being. What makes that person a good choice? Which of that person's qualities would I like to have? How has he or she developed them? (Consider asking him or her.)

_____

_____

_____

What other people have qualities I admire? Can I ask them similar questions?

Confess your sins to each other and pray for each other so that you may be healed. The earnest prayer of a righteous person has great power and produces wonderful results.
JAMES 5:16

Prayer

Pray through the relationships and concerns you listed under the first two questions. Pray that God will move those relationships toward the goals he has for them. Pray for wisdom in developing qualities of courage, humility, and acceptance.

WEEK 6

STEP SIX: We were entirely ready to have God remove these defects of character.

When taking inventory in Step Four, I recalled spheres in which something was wrong. Are there any patterns? Do those problems point out any character defects in me? If so, what are they?

_____

_____

_____

_____

Scripture

Have you forgotten the encouraging words God spoke to you as his children? He said, "My child, don't make light of the LORD's discipline, and don't give up when he corrects you. For the LORD disciplines those he loves, and he punishes each one he accepts as his child." As you endure this divine discipline, remember that God is treating you as his own children. Who ever heard of a child who is never disciplined by its father? If God doesn't discipline you as he does all of his children, it means that you are illegitimate and are not really his children at all. Since we respected our earthly fathers who disciplined us, shouldn't we submit even more to the discipline of the Father of our spirits, and live forever? For our earthly fathers disciplined us for a few years, doing the best they knew how. But God's discipline is always good for us, so that we might share in his holiness. No discipline is enjoyable while it is happening—it's painful! But afterward there will be a peaceful harvest of right living for those who are trained in this way.
HEBREWS 12:5-11

What is one area of my life in which I am aware of God's discipline
at work? How has that discipline brought me closer to being entirely
ready to be changed?

_____

_____

_____

_____

For Reflection

As I think about my particular character defects, what are some
specific instances where they've played out in my life? How did my
defects shape those experiences?

_____

_____

_____

_____

Were they experiences that

- made me angry?
- hurt me?
- I liked but felt guilty about?
- changed my mood instantly?
- made me feel needy?
- pushed me back to my addiction?
- made me relapse into old habits?

Prayer

God, I am not ready for you to do this work in me, but please make
me ready. I can't see the end, but give me the vision or the faith I
need to keep going. I know that I don't recognize all my faults, but

help me to see them clearly. God, I don't know the way out, but give me wisdom. I don't know what I need, but you do. Amen.

WEEK 7

STEP SEVEN: We humbly asked God to remove our shortcomings.

In Step Six, I listed some character defects I could see. Being aware of them can help reduce the influence and power they hold over me. How will I practice being more aware of them in my everyday activities?

_____

_____

_____

Scripture
Dear friends, you always followed my instructions when I was with you. And now that I am away, it is even more important. Work hard to show the results of your salvation, obeying God with deep reverence and fear. For God is working in you, giving you the desire and the power to do what pleases him.
Philippians 2:12-13

God does not force people to do things against their wills. As God is working in me, how will I choose to cooperate with him in working it out?

_____

_____

For Reflection
What relationship has been most affected by my shortcomings?
What have some of the effects been?

_____

_____

_____

_____

Has my relationship experienced these effects?

- isolation from others
- distancing from others
- overdependence
- arguments
- deception
- manipulation
- neglect
- enabling

Prayer
Use the issues raised in each of this week's questions to guide your
conversation with God.

WEEK 8

STEP EIGHT: We made a list of all persons we had harmed and became willing to make amends to them all.

When has someone sought to make amends with me? How did I respond? How did I feel about that person afterward?

_____

_____

_____

_____

Scripture

Jacob looked up and saw Esau coming with his 400 men. . . . As he approached his brother, he bowed to the ground seven times before him. Then Esau ran to meet him and embraced him, threw his arms around his neck, and kissed him. And they both wept.

. . . "And what were all the flocks and herds I met as I came?" Esau asked.

Jacob replied, "They are a gift, my lord, to ensure your friendship."

"My brother, I have plenty," Esau answered. "Keep what you have for yourself."

But Jacob insisted, "No, if I have found favor with you, please accept this gift from me. And what a relief to see your friendly smile. It is like seeing the face of God! Please take this gift I have brought you, for God has been very gracious to me. I have more than enough." And because Jacob insisted, Esau finally accepted the gift.

GENESIS 33:1, 3-4, 8-11

Considering the individuals with whom I plan to make amends, what outcome do I desire for each relationship or each conversation?

What choices can I make for myself that will move me toward that outcome in the relationship?

_____

_____

_____

For Reflection
Perhaps I could start by writing a letter to someone to whom I need to make amends. I don't need to send the letter, but I can sort out my thoughts by putting together a list of things to write about.

Here are a few suggested topics:

- My Feelings
- Your Feelings
- How I Would Feel in Your Position
- What I Would Expect in Your Position
- Reasons for Conflict
- The Outcome I Hope For

_____

_____

_____

Prayer
Pray for each person with whom you need to make amends.

WEEK 9

STEP NINE: We made direct amends to such people wherever possible, except when to do so would injure them or others.

How am I different from the person I was when I made those mistakes that hurt others? How does that make our relationship different now?

_____

_____

_____

Read Step Nine, Day 3 in *The Life Recovery Devotional.*

Scripture

Jesus entered Jericho and made his way through the town. There was a man there named Zacchaeus. He was the chief tax collector in the region, and he had become very rich. He tried to get a look at Jesus, but he was too short to see over the crowd. So he ran ahead and climbed a sycamore-fig tree beside the road, for Jesus was going to pass that way. When Jesus came by, he looked up at Zacchaeus and called him by name. "Zacchaeus!" he said. "Quick, come down! I must be a guest in your home today." Zacchaeus quickly climbed down and took Jesus to his house in great excitement and joy.

But the people were displeased. "He has gone to be the guest of a notorious sinner," they grumbled.

Meanwhile, Zacchaeus stood before the Lord and said, "I will give half my wealth to the poor, Lord, and if I have cheated people on their taxes, I will give them back four times as much!"

Jesus responded, "Salvation has come to this home today, for this man has shown himself to be a true son of Abraham. For the Son of Man came to seek and save those who are lost."
LUKE 19:1-10

In Step Eight, I wrote out some desired outcomes for certain relationships. In order to do my part in making those outcomes realities, what is required of me? What has happened recently that could be an opportunity to put this into practice? What can I begin doing today?

_____

_____

_____

For Reflection
People I've hurt may need to have the relationship mended between us. How will they be better off once I have made amends? Is that a gift I'm willing to give? If not, why not?

_____

_____

_____

Prayer
Ask God to prepare your heart, filling you with courage and humility. Ask God to prepare the hearts of others for acceptance and receptivity. Ask for wisdom about what to say and the attitude in which to say it, and for a mind and heart in tune with him.

WEEK 10

STEP TEN: We continued to take personal inventory, and when we were wrong, promptly admitted it.

By admitting it when I'm wrong, have I felt stronger or weaker? better or worse? more or less pressure? Why have I felt those ways?

_____

_____

_____

Scripture

Since you have heard about Jesus and have learned the truth that comes from him, throw off your old sinful nature and your former way of life, which is corrupted by lust and deception. Instead, let the Spirit renew your thoughts and attitudes. Put on your new nature, created to be like God— truly righteous and holy. So stop telling lies. Let us tell our neighbors the truth, for we are all parts of the same body. And "don't sin by letting anger control you." Don't let the sun go down while you are still angry, for anger gives a foothold to the devil.
EPHESIANS 4:21-27

What footholds—like anger in Ephesians 4:27—do I need to be careful not to give the devil? When I am tempted in those areas, what can I busy myself with instead?

_____

_____

For some ideas, read Ephesians 4:28–
5:4; 5:10-11; and 5:15-20.

For Reflection

In what spheres of my life do I still need to apply these principles? What is holding me back from doing so?

_____

_____

> **Even if I'm not yet ready, what choice could I make that would move me toward becoming ready?**
>
> *I don't mean to say that I have already achieved these things or that I have already reached perfection. But I press on to possess that perfection for which Christ Jesus first possessed me. No, dear brothers and sisters, I have not achieved it, but I focus on this one thing: Forgetting the past and looking forward to what lies ahead, I press on to reach the end of the race and receive the heavenly prize for which God, through Christ Jesus, is calling us.*
> PHILIPPIANS 3:12-14

Prayer

God, I admit that I am weak, but you are strong. I am in need, but you are complete. I am unfinished, but you are working in me. I admit that I cannot continue, but I ask you to continue your work in me until it is finally finished. Amen.

WEEK 11

STEP ELEVEN: We sought through prayer and meditation to improve our conscious contact with God, praying only for knowledge of his will for us and the power to carry it out.

When has God's will been most clear to me? What were the circumstances surrounding that time?

_____

_____

Scripture

I have not stopped thanking God for you. I pray for you constantly, asking God, the glorious Father of our Lord Jesus Christ, to give you spiritual wisdom and insight so that you might grow in your knowledge of God. I pray that your hearts will be flooded with light so that you can understand the confident hope he has given to those he called—his holy people who are his rich and glorious inheritance. I also pray that you will understand the incredible greatness of God's power for us who believe him. This is the same mighty power that raised Christ from the dead and seated him in the place of honor at God's right hand in the heavenly realms.
EPHESIANS 1:16-20

What aspect of God's will is most obvious to me right now? What will it take to carry that out?

_____

_____

For Reflection
What activities besides prayer and meditation might fit my personality to help me connect with God? I can try the various things on my

list and see if they make me more aware of God. I may not always feel like doing those things, but I may find that my feelings follow my choices.

Possibilities could include the following: painting, walking/running, hiking, fishing, reading, serving others, being outdoors, writing, singing or playing music.

_____

_____

_____

> *[Jesus] went on a little farther and bowed*
> *with his face to the ground, praying,*
> *"My Father! If it is possible, let this cup*
> *of suffering be taken away from me. Yet I*
> *want your will to be done, not mine." . . .*
> *Then [he] left [his disciples] a second time*
> *and prayed, "My Father! If this cup cannot*
> *be taken away unless I drink it, your will*
> *be done."*
> MATTHEW 26:39, 42

Prayer
Consider praying through Psalms 27; 65; and 119:1-11.

WEEK 12

STEP TWELVE: Having had a spiritual awakening as the result of these steps, we tried to carry this message to others, and to practice these principles in all our affairs.

As I review my story so far, what are the significant moments that I can share with others beginning their journeys? What are some high and low points in my journey? Both aspects are important in telling my story and in encouraging others in theirs. With whom could I share my story?

_____

_____

_____

_____

Scripture
Dear brothers and sisters, if another believer is overcome by some sin, you who are godly should gently and humbly help that person back onto the right path. And be careful not to fall into the same temptation yourself. Share each other's burdens, and in this way obey the law of Christ. If you think you are too important to help someone, you are only fooling yourself. You are not that important. Pay careful attention to your own work, for then you will get the satisfaction of a job well done, and you won't need to compare yourself to anyone else. For we are each responsible for our own conduct.
GALATIANS 6:1-5

Do I know people who could benefit from starting a journey like this? What would I want to tell them, and how?

_____

_____

For Reflection

What have I learned that I think others could benefit from? What have others taught me that I think would be beneficial for still others to hear? What other people would I like to talk to about their stories?

_____

_____

_____

_____

> Psalm 107:1-32 reviews the stories of God's faithfulness to people who cried out to him, "Lord, help!" How does my own experience illustrate God's faithfulness?

Prayer

God, give me humility and the wisdom to avoid temptation as I seek to help others. Remind me of my own story so that I can be sympathetic toward others. Help me not to become proud of my progress, as if I could not relapse or as if I've progressed all on my own without your help. Amen.

WEEK 13
Recovering My Life

My Story
What have been some significant conversations, realizations, or changes for me so far? Write about those here, or reread the weeks in which they occurred and reflect on them here. What is the value for me of recording those stories? What value is there for others?

My Future
What impact have the changes so far had on my vision moving forward? What seems possible now that didn't seem possible before I started?

As I look at Weeks 7, 8, and 9, how has my attitude changed toward those issues and people? Do those challenges seem bigger or smaller now? Can I see a path toward meeting those challenges?

My Plan

As I move forward in recovery, the next steps for me are

- _____

- _____

- _____

- _____

The next step I plan to take is

_____

_____

Prayer

As I review my prayers so far, these requests still remain true for me today:

_____

_____

_____

SEASON 2

FROM HEART TO SOUL

The heart is where recovery starts. It is in our hearts, in the deepest core of our wills, that we must choose to face the hard acknowledgment that we are powerless. As we work the Twelve Steps, our hearts are continually challenged to will what is right. Will alone, however, is not enough. As everyone in recovery discovers, our wills are hampered by the decisions we have already made and by our thoughts, feelings, and patterns of behavior.

For the last thirteen weeks, you have focused on loving the Lord with all your heart. Next week, you will begin reviewing the Twelve Steps again, this time focusing on loving the Lord with all your soul, with what Dallas Willard, in *The Renovation of the Heart*, calls your "inner stream of life" (Colorado Springs: NavPress, 2002, p. 206), the part of yourself that organizes your will, thoughts, feelings, and behavior. This isn't simply "starting over"; working the Twelve Steps has already started bringing recovery to your life. In Week 13 you summarized the insights and changes brought about by this process. Now it's time to build on those insights and changes. Don't neglect to follow up on the plans you've just made, but allow them to be shaped by what you discover in the coming weeks.

WEEK 1

STEP ONE: We admitted that we were powerless over our problems and that our lives had become unmanageable.

Admitting that something has beaten us runs counter to our pride. But being powerless does not mean being a victim. (See "The Paradox of Powerlessness" on page 1483 in *The Life Recovery Bible*.) How would I describe a specific incident that convinced me of my powerlessness?

_____

_____

_____

Scripture
We now have this light shining in our hearts, but we ourselves are like fragile clay jars containing this great treasure. This makes it clear that our great power is from God, not from ourselves.
2 CORINTHIANS 4:7

Have I ever seen someone like this, who seemed weak and powerless in himself or herself but had the power of God? How would a person like that act?

_____

_____

_____

Have I thought of people from the Bible? from history? from my childhood? from fictional stories?

For Reflection

How have I tried (and failed) to solve my problems in the past?

_____

_____

_____

Look back at your entries for Season 1, Week 1 (pp. 3–5).

Prayer

Lift up your thoughts and concerns about power and powerlessness to God.

WEEK 2

STEP TWO: We came to believe that a Power greater than ourselves could restore us to sanity.

God is in the restoration business. For 99 percent of the Bible (everything after the fall of humanity, in Genesis 3), God is working to restore his creation from the brokenness of sin. What examples from the Bible, from my life, or from the world around me show that God is making things new again?

_____

_____

Here's one example: Read about a
valley of dry bones in Ezekiel 37:1-
14 (pp. 1055–56 in *The Life Recovery
Bible*).

Scripture

*[The woman] thought to herself, "If I can just touch [Jesus'] robe, I will be
healed." Immediately the bleeding stopped, and she could feel in her body
that she had been healed of her terrible condition.*
MARK 5:28-29

What is the equivalent in my life to touching Jesus' robe? How can
I put into action my faith that God's power can restore me?

_____

_____

For Reflection

What would restoration look like in my life? If God changed one
thing about me with a single touch, what would that one thing be?
How would I think and behave differently?

_____

_____

_____

Prayer

Lord, I believe that you are a God who saves and heals. The healing
I desire for my life is this: _____

_____, yet not my will but yours be done. Amen.

WEEK 3

STEP THREE: We made a decision to turn our wills and our lives over to the care of God.

In Step Three, you release your hopes, dreams, choices, addictions, compulsions, and relationships to God's control. This is difficult, especially when life has taught you not to trust people. What were the ups and downs of trust in your relationships over the years? Who could you trust, and who could you not trust in each phase of life?

_____

_____

_____

_____

Phases of Life

- before school age
- early childhood
- preteen years
- high school
- first job

Scripture

[Moses said to the people,] "Now listen! Today I am giving you a choice between life and death, between prosperity and disaster."
DEUTERONOMY 30:15

Do I really think that life is better with God than apart from God?
If not, what keeps me from believing that it is?

_____

_____

_____

For Reflection
What do I fear losing if I turn my life over to God? What is the worst
thing that could happen?

_____

_____

_____

_____

Prayer
God, I want you to be the master of my life. Help me to turn my life
and my will over to your care and protection. Ease my burden, and
help me to overcome my feelings of shame and guilt. Help me to live
a life focused on you and your will for my life. Amen.

WEEK 4

**STEP FOUR: We made a searching and fearless moral inventory
of ourselves.**

Take moral inventory of the last few days.

Have I taken inventory of

- my actions?
- my words?
- my thoughts?
- my emotions?
- my intentions?

Scripture

The kind of sorrow God wants us to experience leads us away from sin and results in salvation. There's no regret for that kind of sorrow. But worldly sorrow, which lacks repentance, results in spiritual death.
2 CORINTHIANS 7:10

For Reflection

Have I felt sorrow in the last few days? If not, when was the last time? What did I do to deal with the sorrow? Was it "the kind of sorrow God wants"?

_____

_____

_____

Prayer

Write a prayer based on your reflections for today.

_____

_____

_____

WEEK 5

STEP FIVE: We admitted to God, to ourselves, and to another human being the exact nature of our wrongs.

Here is what happened when I confessed my wrongs to myself, God, or another person. Were there any times when I should have taken the opportunity to confess, but I didn't?

_____

_____

_____

Scripture

Oh, what joy for those whose disobedience is forgiven, whose sin is put out of sight! Yes, what joy for those whose record the LORD has cleared of guilt, whose lives are lived in complete honesty! When I refused to confess my sin, my body wasted away, and I groaned all day long. Day and night your hand of discipline was heavy on me. My strength evaporated like water in the summer heat. . . . Finally, I confessed all my sins to you and stopped trying to hide my guilt. I said to myself, "I will confess my rebellion to the LORD." And you forgave me! All my guilt is gone.
PSALM 32:1-5

For Reflection

What is the one thing I found in my moral inventory that I decided never to tell another human being? What would I say if I were to actually confess this one most shameful thing? What words would I use to confess it?

_____

_____

_____

Read about honesty on page 701
of *The Life Recovery Bible.*

Prayer
God, I must confess to you these things:

_____

_____

_____

WEEK 6

STEP SIX: We were entirely ready to have God remove these defects of character.

A lot of our flaws are coping mechanisms that we use to help ourselves get through life. How did I get through the last few days? Were there any situations in which a character flaw actually helped me? How did it hurt me (and others)?

Do any of these words apply?

- reject
- ignore
- fight
- cover up
- lie
- blame

- accept
- please
- scare
- impress
- withdraw
- distract

Scripture

The sacrifice you desire is a broken spirit. You will not reject a broken and repentant heart, O God.
PSALM 51:17

For Reflection

What "sacrifices" do I bring before God and people to make up for my sins? In the last few days, how have I tried to pay for my sins myself? What is the difference between offering God a sacrifice and offering him a broken and repentant heart?

Prayer

Write out a prayer about your defects of character. Use Psalm 51 as a guide, if you like.

_____

_____

_____

WEEK 7

STEP SEVEN: We humbly asked God to remove our shortcomings.

"We can ask God to change our attitudes. When he deals with our pride, we will be able to stop hiding behind our reputation. We can allow ourselves to become 'anonymous,' each of us known as just another person struggling with addiction" (See "Into the Open," *The Life Recovery Bible*, p. 1523). How does this quote intersect with my life in the last few days?

_____

_____

_____

Scripture

Give us today the food we need, and forgive us our sins, as we have forgiven those who sin against us. And don't let us yield to temptation, but rescue us from the evil one.

MATTHEW 6:11-13

For Reflection

When Jesus taught his followers how to pray for their own needs, he told them to depend on God each day for food, forgiveness, and freedom from evil (see Matthew 6:11-13). How do I feel about the idea of asking God for the same thing every day? In what ways am I depending on him? How often and in what ways do I acknowledge my dependence on him?

Do any of these words fit in my answer?

- humbled
- humiliated
- peaceful
- angry
- forget
- remind
- tired
- habit
- afraid

Prayer

Write out a prayer using the Lord's Prayer as a guide (see Matthew 6:9-13).

WEEK 8

STEP EIGHT: We made a list of all persons we had harmed and became willing to make amends to them all.

If I were to make a list of the people I have harmed today, who would be on it? What about this week? the last few months? Describe some of the specific incidents in which these people were harmed.

_____

_____

_____

_____

_____

Scripture

Plant the good seeds of righteousness, and you will harvest a crop of love. Plow up the hard ground of your hearts, for now is the time to seek the LORD, that he may come and shower righteousness upon you.
HOSEA 10:12

This step is never easy; it reminds us of things we would rather avoid thinking about. How is this experience like plowing up hard ground? Describe your thoughts and feelings about this experience.

_____

_____

_____

_____

For Reflection

What other images fit how this step
makes me feel:

- sinking lower and lower into the
  ground?
- shrinking smaller and smaller?
- cleaning up a messy room?

Working this step is like

_____

_____.

Prayer
God, help me to be honest and fearless as I work this step. Amen.

WEEK 9

STEP NINE: We made direct amends to such people wherever possible, except when to do so would injure them or others.

How does this step intersect with my life in the last few days?

_____

_____

_____

Would it help me to reflect on the last few days by answering these questions?

- Where did I spend my time?
- With whom did I talk?
- What were my activities?
- What was I thinking about?
- How did I feel?
- What was the high point/low point?

_____

_____

_____

_____

_____

Scripture

If you are presenting a sacrifice at the altar in the Temple and you suddenly remember that someone has something against you, leave your sacrifice there at the altar. Go and be reconciled to that person. Then come and offer your sacrifice to God.
MATTHEW 5:23-24

Am I motivated to reconcile with other people, or would I rather just try to forget about the problems between us? What *does* motivate me to make peace? What motivation does this passage from Matthew provide?

_____

_____

_____

_____

For Reflection

Making amends isn't about me. It's not about getting something off my chest or making people see how far I've come in recovery. In order to truly make amends, I have to put the interests of others ahead of my own interests (see Philippians 2:4). What will it be like to make amends to the specific people mentioned in last week's entry? What will make it difficult? What will make it easier? What will my motivation be?

_____

_____

_____

_____

_____

Prayer

Lord, I need to be at peace with you, but you want me to be at peace with the people to whom I need to make amends. I offer up to you my relationship with these people: _____ _____. Give me the strength I need to face the problems in my relationships with them. Amen.

WEEK 10

STEP TEN: We continued to take personal inventory, and when we were wrong, promptly admitted it.

What was a specific incident in which I refused to admit that I was wrong? What were the consequences? How does this incident compare with my behavior in the last few days?

_____

_____

_____

_____

"Pride whispers to us, 'Don't worry, you can handle this one; you're not like those addicts anymore'" (*The Life Recovery Devotional*, Step Ten, Day 4).

Scripture
You have charged us to keep your commandments carefully. Oh, that my actions would consistently reflect your decrees! Then I will not be ashamed when I compare my life with your commands.
PSALM 119:4-6

For Reflection
What would my life look like if I consistently followed God's decrees? What have been some of my attitudes, actions, and reactions over the last few days? And what would they have looked like if my life had lined up with God's commands?

_____

_____

_____

_____

Prayer

Lord, I admit that these are some of the ways I have been wrong in the last few days: _____
_____. As the psalmist prayed, "Keep me from lying to myself; give me the privilege of knowing your instructions" (Psalm 119:29). Amen.

WEEK 11

STEP ELEVEN: We sought through prayer and meditation to improve our conscious contact with God, praying only for knowledge of his will for us and the power to carry it out.

When have I been most conscious of contact with God? Is there a specific incident? How does that incident compare with my life over the last couple of days?

_____

_____

_____

_____

Scripture

Oh, the joys of those who do not follow the advice of the wicked, or stand around with sinners, or join in with mockers. But they delight in the law of the LORD, meditating on it day and night. They are like trees planted along the riverbank, bearing fruit each season. Their leaves never wither, and they prosper in all they do.
PSALM 1:1-3

For Reflection

For the psalmist, meditating on God's law meant reciting to himself the commands from the five books of Moses (Genesis, Exodus, Leviticus, Numbers, and Deuteronomy). What does meditating look like for me? What ways have I used to meditate on God's commands? How have I seen other people do it?

_____

_____

_____

_____

Here are some passages of Scripture to meditate on or to memorize:

- The Ten Commandments (Exodus 20:1-17; Deuteronomy 5:6-21)
- Deuteronomy 6:4-9
- Psalm 1
- Psalm 119
- Isaiah 1:11-20
- The Sermon on the Mount (Matthew 5–7)
- The Most Important Commandments (Mark 12:29-31)
- Romans 12

- Philippians 2:1-18
- Hebrews 12
- James 1

Prayer

Teach me your decrees, O LORD;
I will keep them to the end.
Give me understanding and I will obey your instructions;
I will put them into practice with all my heart.
Make me walk along the path of your commands,
for that is where my happiness is found.
Give me an eagerness for your laws
rather than a love for money!
Turn my eyes from worthless things,
and give me life through your word.
Reassure me of your promise,
made to those who fear you.
Help me abandon my shameful ways;
for your regulations are good.
I long to obey your commandments!
Renew my life with your goodness.
PSALM 119:33-40

WEEK 12

STEP TWELVE: Having had a spiritual awakening as the result of these steps, we tried to carry this message to others and to practice these principles in all our affairs.

In what ways have I had a spiritual awakening? How was I spiritually asleep before working through these steps? In what areas of my life am I still asleep—not practicing these principles?

_____

_____

_____

_____

_____

> If I can't think of any areas in which
> I'm failing to practice these principles,
> I will ask my sponsor or someone else
> who knows me well.

Scripture
The Spirit of the Sovereign LORD is upon me, for the LORD has anointed me to bring good news to the poor. He has sent me to comfort the brokenhearted and to proclaim that captives will be released and prisoners will be freed.
ISAIAH 61:1

How does my life fit this verse? In what ways have I been poor, brokenhearted, or a captive? In what ways have I been the one with the Lord's Spirit upon me?

_____

_____

_____

For Reflection
What will my life look like when I am more mature in recovery? What kinds of specific acts will I perform? What kinds of responses will I have to my own problems and to others' problems?

_____

_____

_____

If you're stuck, try thinking of an incident in which you were unhappy with your reactions to certain problems. How would a more mature "you" have reacted? Write out those actions.

Prayer
Write a prayer that lifts up to God your gratitude and your concerns about your maturity in recovery.

_____

_____

_____

WEEK 13
Recovering My Life

My Story
Looking over the journal entries for the last twelve weeks, what do
I see as the most important events and realizations? What important events and realizations happened that aren't mentioned in my
journal?

_____

_____

_____

_____

When I compare "My Story" on page 27 (from the first season) with
the one above, what has been added since then? How would I tell it
differently now?

_____

_____

_____

_____

My Future
Looking over the journal entries from this season, what ideas do I
get about what my future could be like? (Try Weeks 1, 2, 5, 9, 10,
11, and 12.) What do I imagine my life may be like when I am more
mature in recovery?

_____

_____

_____

My Plan

What action steps can I take to move toward the future I have envisioned?

- _____

- _____

- _____

- _____

Look back at "My Plan" on page 28 (from Season 1, Week 13). Have I carried out these plans? Are there parts of these plans that I still need to carry out? parts that I need to revise or drop?

_____

_____

_____

Prayer

Write a prayer based on your reflections for today.

_____

_____

_____

SEASON 3

FROM SOUL TO MIND

Addiction affects the whole person, but its effects on the addict's mind are especially evident. Dependence creates unhealthy patterns of thinking and feeling that we continue to deal with throughout the process of recovery. Perhaps even more powerful than these thoughts and feelings are the images we carry in our minds—images that define who we are, what our story is, and who God is. For example, we may cherish images of ourselves as fiercely independent people who don't rely on God or other people to get by. We may picture God as the ultimate "religious" person: sheltered, joyless, and interested only in religious people. Even after we have acknowledged that we rely on our addictions and that our lives have become unmanageable, we still may cling to the image of our independence. We may continue to keep our distance from God because of how we perceive him.

   The collection of thoughts, feelings, and images that make up the mind must be restored to sanity. As you work the Twelve Steps again in the coming season, pay particular attention to how each step intersects with your mind. Think about the sane thoughts, feelings, and images that you want to have in place of your addictive ones. Love God with all your mind.

WEEK 1

STEP ONE: We admitted that we were powerless over our problems and that our lives had become unmanageable.

We turn to addictive behaviors and substances to help us cope with problems in our lives. But the benefits are short lived and counter-productive; the end result is alienation and loneliness. What personal problems was I originally trying to escape when I became addicted?

Scripture

Deeper and deeper I sink into the mire; I can't find a foothold. I am in deep water, and the floods overwhelm me.
PSALM 69:2

How does this verse describe my experience?

For Reflection

What new problems, losses, and/or alienations have resulted from my wrong choices?

Have I read Job's take on human
weakness in Job 14:1-6 (p. 650 in
The Life Recovery Bible)? How might I
describe my life using Job's words?

Prayer
God, I am powerless and weak. I long for your power to fill me as I
begin the process of recovery. Please correct my thoughts and feelings so that I may start healing the hurts I have caused. Fill me with
your Spirit every day. Amen.

WEEK 2

**STEP TWO: We came to believe that a Power greater than ourselves
could restore us to sanity.**

In his book *Renovation of the Heart* Dallas Willard says, "The single
most important thing in our mind is our idea of God and the associ-
ated images" (Colorado Springs: NavPress, 2002, p. 100). If I were to
paint a picture of God, what would it look like? What would he be
doing? What else would be in the picture?

_____

_____

_____

_____

How would I picture God's

- wisdom?
- power?
- love?
- mercy?
- faithfulness?

Scripture

You asked, "Who is this that questions my wisdom with such ignorance?"
It is I—and I was talking about things I knew nothing about, things far too
wonderful for me.
JOB 42:3

What questions do I have for God? What is the difference between
asking legitimate questions and "questioning God's wisdom"?

_____

_____

_____

For Reflection

If God were to paint a picture of me, what would I be doing?

_____

_____

_____

How do I feel about that image?

Prayer
God, help me to believe in you. Help me to trust in your ability to restore sane thoughts and emotions to my life so that I may experience healing. Give me wisdom and understanding about you, and draw me close to you. Help me not to question your wisdom. Give me insight into the bigger picture so that I may change and become more like you. Amen.

WEEK 3

STEP THREE: We made a decision to turn our wills and our lives over to the care of God.

Turning over control of our lives is easier when we remember that our sense of having control is only an illusion. We have thought that we were the masters of our lives, but our problems have mastered us. What behaviors and experiences make me feel as if I am in charge of my life? What experiences show that I am not in charge?

_____

_____

_____

Scripture
Jesus said, "Come to me, all of you who are weary and carry heavy burdens, and I will give you rest. Take my yoke upon you. Let me teach you, because I am humble and gentle at heart, and you will find rest for your souls. For my yoke is easy to bear, and the burden I give you is light."
MATTHEW 11:28-30

What thoughts and attitudes burden me and others around me? How are those thoughts and attitudes controlling me?

_____

_____

_____

_____

For Reflection
What has God taught me about turning over my will to him? When have I been able to learn from Jesus?

_____

_____

_____

After reading "Single-Minded Devotion" on page 1607 of *The Life Recovery Bible*, how do I feel about turning my will over to God?

Prayer
God, I give you my life and my will. Help me to serve you in my thoughts, feelings, and actions. Help me to throw off my old sinful nature. Give me the strength to pray every day to align my will with yours. Amen.

WEEK 4

STEP FOUR: We made a searching and fearless moral inventory of ourselves.

Many of us have spent our lives in hiding, ashamed of who we are inside. When we *do* dig deep, we uncover a lot of dirt in our lives; sometimes thoughts and feelings surface that we didn't know were there. What problems/thoughts/feelings have I been hiding from others? from myself?

_____

_____

Scripture
Though your sins are like scarlet, I will make them as white as snow. Though they are red like crimson, I will make them as white as wool.
ISAIAH 1:18

Do I believe the truth of this verse? How does it make me feel in light of my personal inventory?

_____

_____

_____

For Reflection
Looking at my personal inventory can be discouraging. How does my personal inventory make me feel about myself? How can God help me to overcome those feelings?

_____

_____

In response to the Israelites' discouragement over their sin, and their
subsequent repentance, Nehemiah
told them, "This is a sacred day
before our LORD. Don't be dejected
and sad, for the joy of the LORD is
your strength" (Nehemiah 8:10).
What would it look like for the joy
of the Lord to be my strength?

Prayer
God, you see everything I've done. Forgive me for each of these
wrongs: _____
_____. Help me to overcome my feelings of guilt and
anxiety and to turn onto your path toward healing. Thank you for
forgiving me and washing away my sins. Amen.

WEEK 5

**STEP FIVE: We admitted to God, to ourselves, and to another human
being the exact nature of our wrongs.**

Vulnerability is a vital part of the healing process. It allows us to be
accepted by another human being and to recognize that peace of
mind comes from revealing who we really are to others and to God.
What parts of my personal inventory stand in the way of my being

able to be vulnerable with God, myself, and others? What are my fears about letting others see who I really am?

_____

_____

_____

Having read "Feelings of Shame" on page 1353 of *The Life Recovery Bible*, in whom can I confide about my thoughts and feelings? What makes that person trustworthy?

Scripture

This is a trustworthy saying, and everyone should accept it: "Christ Jesus came into the world to save sinners"—and I am the worst of them all. But God had mercy on me so that Christ Jesus could use me as a prime example of his great patience with even the worst sinners. Then others will realize that they, too, can believe in him and receive eternal life. 1 TIMOTHY 1:15-16

Paul considered himself the worst sinner because he had participated in the persecution and murder of Christians before he himself became a Christian. How does this passage give me the courage to share my moral inventory with God, myself, and others?

_____

_____

_____

For Reflection

God wants me to confess my sins to him and to others so that I can receive forgiveness. I may feel ashamed of what I've done, but God and others are waiting to forgive me. There is no sin too great for God to forgive. How can I start to overcome my shame today? How does God's offer of mercy and forgiveness make me feel?

_____

_____

_____

Prayer

Lord God, do not allow my feelings of shame to get in the way of my process of recovery. Help me to overcome my fear of sharing with others what I've done. Show me someone in whom I can confide. Please bring me peace of mind. Allow me to accept your forgiveness and the forgiveness of others. Thank you for forgiving my sins and for forgetting them. Help me to continue confessing new sins and not to retreat into myself again. Amen.

WEEK 6

STEP SIX: We were entirely ready to have God remove these defects of character.

Addictions are a shelter; removal of that shelter can reveal the deeper problems that lie underneath. What deeper problems—especially concerning thoughts and feelings—lie underneath my addiction shelter?

_____

_____

Scripture

When I refused to confess my sin, my body wasted away, and I groaned all day long. Day and night your hand of discipline was heavy on me. My strength evaporated like water in the summer heat. Finally, I confessed all my sins to you and stopped trying to hide my guilt. I said to myself, "I will confess my rebellion to the LORD." And you forgave me! All my guilt is gone. PSALM 32:3-5

As I begin the process of turning my defective thoughts and feelings over to God, how are these verses from Psalm 32 a source of comfort?

_____

_____

_____

For Reflection

Part of the battle I face with my thoughts is about making wrong choices. How can I start changing my thoughts so that I make right choices instead of wrong choices? How can I turn my thoughts, feelings, and actions over to God today?

_____

_____

_____

_____

> God wants us to mourn over our
> sins and admit our brokenness. How
> will that help me give my defective
> thoughts and feelings to God?

Prayer

Write a prayer below. Admit your defects to God, and boldly ask him
to remove each one.

_____

_____

_____

_____

WEEK 7

STEP SEVEN: We humbly asked God to remove our shortcomings.

Humility is the key to successfully completing this step. But humility
is very different from humiliation. What is humility? How do I put
humility into practice?

_____

_____

_____

_____

To help you process your feelings
about humility, read "A Humble
Heart" on page 1323 of _The Life
Recovery Bible._

Scripture

[Jesus] was despised and rejected—a man of sorrows, acquainted with deepest grief. We turned our backs on him and looked the other way. He was despised, and we did not care. Yet it was our weaknesses he carried; it was our sorrows that weighed him down. And we thought his troubles were a punishment from God, a punishment for his own sins! But he was pierced for our rebellion, crushed for our sins. He was beaten so we could be whole. He was whipped so we could be healed.
ISAIAH 53:3-5

My sins, no matter how great, are already forgiven because of Jesus' perfect sacrifice. Does that knowledge make it easier or harder to ask God to remove my shortcomings? Why do I feel that way?

For Reflection

This step is a turning point in the recovery process, a time to reflect on where I've been and to make the move toward acting on the person I should become. In what ways am I ready to take this step this week? In what ways am I not ready?

Prayer

God, thank you for being in charge of my life. Help me to trust you. I come before you in complete humility. Please help me to identify and turn over all my shortcomings to you. Help me to practice humility toward others. Thank you for Jesus' sacrifice and for the forgiveness of my sins. Help me to accept that forgiveness and to

become more like you, conforming my will to your will every day.
In Jesus' name I pray, Amen.

WEEK 8

**STEP EIGHT: We made a list of all persons we had harmed and
became willing to make amends to them all.**

Write down the name of each person (including yourself) to whom
you need to make amends. Imagine how each person will react when
you approach him or her to make amends. Describe that reaction.
How does that make you feel?

_____

_____

_____

Scripture

*I am not overstating it when I say that the man who caused all the
trouble hurt all of you more than he hurt me. . . . Now, however, it is
time to forgive and comfort him. Otherwise he may be overcome by
discouragement. So I urge you now to reaffirm your love for him.*
2 CORINTHIANS 2:5, 7-8

How can I keep from being overcome by feelings of discouragement
as I prepare to face the people I have hurt?

_____

_____

For Reflection

As I created the list of people I have hurt, I was reminded of the ways they have hurt *me* as well. How can I keep from harboring resentment toward those people? What steps will I take in order to become willing to make amends to them?

_____

_____

_____

_____

Read and reflect on the implications
of Matthew 6:14-15.

Prayer

Jesus, I have hurt many people, but most of all, I have hurt you. Thank you for forgiving me. Allow me to be honest with myself so that I can remember everyone I have wronged. Give me the courage to be willing to make amends to those I have hurt. Help me to graciously accept their responses, whatever they are. Keep me from being resentful toward those I have hurt and help me to forgive them for any wrongs they have committed against me, just as you have forgiven me. Grant me your grace and mercy as I continue on my road to recovery. Amen.

WEEK 9

STEP NINE: We made direct amends to such people wherever possible, except when to do so would injure them or others.

Making amends to the people we have hurt can be very scary. Describe your emotions as you go through the process of opening the lines of communication with those you have hurt.

_____

_____

_____

How can I rely on God to get me through the process of making amends?

_____

_____

_____

_____

Scripture

Suppose I tell some wicked people that they will surely die, but then they turn from their sins and do what is just and right. For instance, they might give back a debtor's security, return what they have stolen, and obey my life-giving laws, no longer doing what is evil. If they do this, then they will surely live and not die. None of their past sins will be brought up again, for they have done what is just and right, and they will surely live.
EZEKIEL 33:14-16

How is this passage a source of comfort as I make amends?

_____

_____

_____

For Reflection

What has been the result of my making amends with each person? What feelings, both good and bad, have I experienced?

_____

_____

_____

_____

Prayer

Write a prayer focusing on those to whom you are making amends. Pray specifically for what you hope to accomplish in each relationship and what you hope that relationship will look like both now and in the future.

_____

_____

_____

_____

WEEK 10

STEP TEN: We continued to take personal inventory, and when we were wrong, promptly admitted it.

Our repeated failures afford us repeated opportunities for healing and growth. How does this encourage me in my recovery?

_____

_____

_____

Scripture
Get rid of all bitterness, rage, anger, harsh words, and slander, as well as all types of evil behavior. Instead, be kind to each other, tenderhearted, forgiving one another, just as God through Christ has forgiven you.
EPHESIANS 4:31-32

What do I need to do in order to get rid of the evil behaviors in my life?

_____

_____

_____

For Reflection
What emotions recently set me back in my recovery? How can I best work through them?

_____

_____

_____

Read "Repeated Forgiveness" on page
1441 of *The Life Recovery Bible*. How
can I apply that idea to my life?

Prayer

God, help me to rely on you in my recovery. Give me the strength
to be more open and honest. Help me to continue to take personal
inventory and to be able to admit when I am wrong so that I can
take steps to immediately correct the situation. Open my heart to
your healing touch. Calm my emotions. Allow me to think clearly
and rationally. Come close to me as I come close to you. Thank you
for your love and forgiveness. Amen.

WEEK 11

**STEP ELEVEN: We sought through prayer and meditation to improve
our conscious contact with God, praying only for knowledge of his
will for us and the power to carry it out.**

Most of us need to desire something before we will seek it wholeheartedly. If we don't believe God truly cares about every detail of
our lives, we are less willing to pray to him. We are too ashamed to
come to him because we don't fully believe he has forgiven our sins.
How can I overcome my feelings of shame and strengthen my desire
to come to God in prayer?

Having read "Thirst for God" on page
697 of *The Life Recovery Bible*, how can
I desire God?

Scripture

Trust in the Lord *with all your heart; do not depend on your own*
understanding. Seek his will in all you do, and he will show you which
path to take.
Proverbs 3:5-6

How do these verses help me understand God's will for my life?
How will seeking God's will help me shape a better future?

_____

_____

_____

For Reflection

When have I turned to God for guidance in the past? What has he
shown me when I have done so?

_____

_____

_____

Prayer

God, I desire to know your will for my life. Help me to understand
what it is you want me to do. Give me the strength to receive your
wisdom and to carry out your plans for me every day. Help me to
seek after you wholeheartedly, no matter how I feel. Show me your
ways, and help me to walk in them. Amen.

WEEK 12

STEP TWELVE: Having had a spiritual awakening as the result of these steps, we tried to carry this message to others, and to practice these principles in all our affairs.

Look over the first eleven steps, and trace your emotional journey to this point. What principles have you learned? How can you apply those principles to your daily life?

_____

_____

_____

_____

Scripture

Just as you accepted Christ Jesus as your Lord, you must continue to follow him. Let your roots grow down into him, and let your lives be built on him. Then your faith will grow strong in the truth you were taught, and you will overflow with thankfulness.
COLOSSIANS 2:6-7

How do these verses help me as I apply what I have learned in the areas of my thoughts and my emotions?

_____

_____

_____

For Reflection

In order to help others on the road to recovery, it is vital that we do not forget what we went through to get to where we are today. Make a list of the positive and negative emotions you have experienced on your journey. How have they shaped who you are today?

_____

_____

_____

_____

_____

_____

> As I reflect on my thoughts and feelings, where do I currently see myself on my journey with God?

Prayer

God, you know my past. Help me to truly overcome it. Give me the strength to apply what I have learned to my life so that I can tell others about what you have done for me. Guard me from any temptations that may come my way. Draw me closer to you. Amen.

WEEK 13
Recovering My Life

My Story

Write an outline of your story. What were the key events; who were key players? What emotional and relational conflicts were involved? What role did the Twelve Steps play?

_____

_____

_____

_____

_____

_____

_____

_____

My Future

Most people can't even imagine what they would be like without their faults. What would you be like? Imagine yourself as someone who isn't tempted with the negative thoughts and feelings you currently have. Write down what that would look like.

_____

_____

_____

_____

My Plan

Set and write down realistic goals for changing your thoughts and feelings one small step at a time. Refer to those goals often to check your emotional progress. Share your goals with others you trust to hold you accountable.

_____

_____

_____

Prayer

God, thank you for helping me on the road to recovery. As I continue to refine my life, help me to remember where I came from and to be willing to continue changing into the person you want me to be. Help me to live my life in a way that is honoring and pleasing to you. I want to glorify you in everything I do. Keep me from the temptation to go back to my old ways of thinking and feeling. Guard me from my destructive ways. Continue to guide me on your path to freedom. I want to be more like you. Conform my will to your will every day, and help me to live my life as a new creation in you. Thank you for your love and acceptance. In Jesus' name, Amen.

FROM MIND TO STRENGTH

You have walked through three-quarters of a year with the Twelve Steps, examining your life through the lenses of the heart, the soul, and the mind. One last season—and one last metaphor for your life—remains: strength.

Your strength includes your physical body. Addiction takes its toll in this realm as well, reorienting the body's internal chemistry toward the addiction and perhaps leaving physical scars in its wake. Many people think of God as too spiritual to be concerned with mere physical bodies. But because God is concerned about your whole person, not just the parts of you that are invisible, he wants to restore your body to health (sanity) as well.

Strength in the biblical sense is not just your physical body, however. It includes all the resources you have: things like money, your relationships, your time, and your abilities and talents. As you work the Twelve Steps this season, pay close attention to the ways in which your body and your resources are tied down by addiction. Focus your prayers and plans on loving God with all your strength instead of wasting your strength on addiction.

WEEK 1

STEP ONE: We admitted that we were powerless over our problems and that our lives had become unmanageable.

"Jesus tells us that in order to enter the Kingdom of God we must become like little children, and this involves being powerless. . . . Little children are singularly reliant on the love, care, and nurture of adults for their most basic needs. They *must* trust their lives to some-one who is more powerful than they are. Although they may not know exactly what they need, they *must* cry out to obtain it, and, hopefully, they will be heard and lovingly cared for" ("Like Little Children," *The Life Recovery Bible*, p. 1267). When have I been forced to trust others? How did those situations turn out? Is trusting God similar to or different from those experiences?

_____

_____

_____

_____

Scripture
[Jesus] said to them, "Let the children come to me. Don't stop them! For the Kingdom of God belongs to those who are like these children. I tell you the truth, anyone who doesn't receive the Kingdom of God like a child will never enter it."
MARK 10:14-15

In what ways am I "like a child"? In what ways do I need to become like one? What aspect of this teaching is hard for me?

_____

_____

_____

_____

Think about what life was like for you
as a child or what life is like for the
children you know. Think of words
that describe their characteristics
(e.g., small, dependent, trusting).

For Reflection
What am I struggling with today? How can I trust God about it?

_____

_____

_____

Prayer
O Father, Lord of heaven and earth, thank you for hiding these
things from those who think themselves wise and clever, and for
revealing them to the childlike. Yes, Father, it pleased you to do it
this way! (Matthew 11:25-26)

WEEK 2

STEP TWO: We came to believe that a Power greater than ourselves could restore us to sanity.

"Saying that we 'came to believe' suggests a process. Belief is the result of consideration, doubt, reasoning, and concluding" ("Coming to Believe," *The Life Recovery Bible*, p. 1431). What specific steps in the considering, doubting, reasoning, concluding process have I taken? Am I convinced that a Power greater than myself can restore me to sanity? What steps do I still need to take?

_____

_____

_____

_____

_____

_____

For ideas, read the rest of "Coming to Believe" on page 1431 of *The Life Recovery Bible.*

Scripture

Faith shows the reality of what we hope for; it is the evidence of things we cannot see. Through their faith, the people in days of old earned a good reputation.
Hebrews 11:1-2

How can hope for a better life (either one like a time in the past or a better future) and the example of other people who have experienced recovery lead me toward my own goal of recovery?

_____

_____

For Reflection

Step Two is often called "the hope step." What specific goals do I hope to reach in my recovery? What will my life look like when I reach those goals? Who will be with me?

_____

_____

_____

_____

Prayer

Because of our faith, Christ has brought us into this place of undeserved privilege where we now stand, and we confidently and joyfully look forward to sharing God's glory. We can rejoice, too, when we run into problems and trials, for we know that they help us develop endurance. And endurance develops strength of character, and character strengthens our confident hope of salvation. And this hope will not lead to disappointment. For we know how dearly God loves us, because he has given us the Holy Spirit to fill our hearts with his love (Romans 5:2-5).

WEEK 3

STEP THREE: We made a decision to turn our wills and our lives over to the care of God.

Describe a life completely turned over to God. What would it look like? How does your life measure up to this image?

_____

_____

_____

_____

For more ideas, read Hebrews 11, a
description of people faithful to God.

Scripture

Dear brothers and sisters, I plead with you to give your bodies to God because of all he has done for you. Let them be a living and holy sacrifice— the kind he will find acceptable. This is truly the way to worship him. Don't copy the behavior and customs of this world, but let God transform you into a new person by changing the way you think. Then you will learn to know God's will for you, which is good and pleasing and perfect.
ROMANS 12:1-2

How would your life be different if you were to turn it completely over to God? Is this an attractive notion to you? Why or why not?

_____

_____

_____

_____

_____

For Reflection

How have I seen God's faithfulness (to me or to others)? What evidence have I seen that life with God is better?

_____

_____

_____

_____

Prayer

Take my life and let it be
Consecrated, Lord, to Thee;
Take my moments and my days—
Let them flow in ceaseless praise.

Take my hands and let them move
At the impulse of Thy love;
Take my feet and let them be
Swift and beautiful for Thee.

Take my voice and let me sing
Always, only, for my King;
Take my lips and let them be
Filled with messages from Thee.

Take my silver and my gold—
Not a mite would I withhold;
Take my intellect and use
Every power as Thou shalt choose.

Take my will and make it Thine—
It shall be no longer mine;
Take my heart—it is Thine own,
It shall be Thy royal throne.

Take my love—my Lord, I pour
At Thy feet its treasure store;
Take myself—and I will be
Ever, only, all for Thee.
—FRANCES RIDLEY HAVERGAL, 1874

WEEK 4

STEP FOUR: We made a searching and fearless moral inventory of ourselves.

"[Making an inventory is] like sifting through all the garbage in our past. This is painful, but it is a necessary part of throwing away those rotten habits and behaviors that, if not dealt with, will almost certainly spoil the rest of our life" ("Confession," *The Life Recovery Bible*, p. 613). In sorting through my habits and behaviors, which of them are worth keeping? Which of them need to be thrown away?

_____

_____

_____

Scripture
Since we are surrounded by such a huge crowd of witnesses to the life of faith, let us strip off every weight that slows us down, especially the sin that so easily trips us up. And let us run with endurance the race God has set before us.
HEBREWS 12:1

How have the habits and behaviors from the last question slowed me down or tripped me up? Are they sinful habits and behaviors? Are they just unhealthy or unhelpful?

_____

_____

_____

For Reflection
What safeguards can I put in place, and what steps can I take to ensure that I continue on the path toward recovery and don't fall back into the actions for which I am sorry?

_____

_____

_____

Think of how those who know you best—your parents, family, and friends—would answer this question about you; or, ask them for their input.

Prayer
The faithful love of the LORD never ends! His mercies never cease. Great is his faithfulness; his mercies begin afresh each morning. . . .

Though he brings grief, he also shows compassion because of the greatness of his unfailing love. For he does not enjoy hurting people or causing them sorrow (Lamentations 3:22-23, 32-33).

WEEK 5

STEP FIVE: We admitted to God, to ourselves, and to another human being the exact nature of our wrongs.

"There is no real freedom without confession. What a relief it is to finally give up the weight of our lies and excuses. When we confess our sins, we will find the internal peace we lost so long ago. We will also be one step closer to recovery" ("Freedom through Confession," *The Life Recovery Bible*, p. 1433). What do I think of this statement? Is it true? What is it like when I confess?

_____

_____

_____

_____

Think of a time when you've confessed your sins or shortcomings. How did you feel afterward? How did the one you confessed to respond?

Scripture

If we claim we have no sin, we are only fooling ourselves and not living in the truth. But if we confess our sins to him, he is faithful and just to forgive us our sins and to cleanse us from all wickedness.
1 JOHN 1:8-9

Why is confession an important part of recovery?

_____

_____

_____

Confess your sins to each other and pray for each other so that you may be healed. The earnest prayer of a righteous person has great power and produces wonderful results.
JAMES 5:16

For Reflection

How can I practice confession as a discipline in my life? To whom can I confess? Who can confess to me? How can this lead me further on the path to recovery?

_____

_____

_____

_____

Prayer

Just as I am, without one plea,
But that Thy blood was shed for me,
And that Thou bidd'st me come to Thee,
O Lamb of God I come! I come!

Just as I am, and waiting not
To rid my soul of one dark blot
To Thee, whose blood can cleanse each spot,
O Lamb of God, I come! I come!
—CHARLOTTE ELLIOTT, 1835

WEEK 6

STEP SIX: We were entirely ready to have God remove these defects of character.

What would it look like if God were to remove my defects of character? How would my life be different?

_____

_____

_____

Scripture
Seek the LORD while you can find him. Call on him now while he is near. Let the wicked change their ways and banish the very thought of doing wrong. Let them turn to the LORD that he may have mercy on them. Yes, turn to our God, for he will forgive generously.
ISAIAH 55:6-7

Part of being ready to have God forgive you is to change your ways and "banish the very thought of doing wrong." In this sense, am I ready for God to cleanse me? If not, what steps can I take to become ready? If I am ready, how can I help others on their recovery journeys?

_____

_____

_____

_____

For Reflection
Allowing God to cleanse us is a process. What am I ready for him to
cleanse now? What do I expect to let him cleanse in the future?

_____

_____

_____

Revisit your entry for Season 4, Week
4 (pp. 89–91). In view of your moral
inventory, what do you need to be
cleansed from?

_____

_____

_____

_____

Prayer
Lord Jesus, I long to be perfectly whole;
I want Thee forever to live in my soul.
Break down every idol, cast out every foe;
Now wash me and I shall be whiter than snow.
—JAMES L. NICHOLSON, 1872

WEEK 7

STEP SEVEN: We humbly asked God to remove our shortcomings.

"When we come to [God] with humility, admitting that we still struggle with many of our shortcomings, he refreshes us and gives us the courage we need to continue the battle" ("Clearing the Mess," *The Life Recovery Bible*, p. 915). In what aspects of my life do I need the courage to keep fighting? Why is this battle so difficult?

_____

_____

_____

_____

If you get stuck, list the patterns of behavior that you can easily fall back into. What makes these habits such frequent pitfalls?

Scripture

Keep on asking, and you will receive what you ask for. Keep on seeking, and you will find. Keep on knocking, and the door will be opened to you. For everyone who asks, receives. Everyone who seeks, finds. And to everyone who knocks, the door will be opened. You parents—if your children ask for a loaf of bread, do you give them a stone instead? Or if they ask for a fish, do you give them a snake? Of course not! So if you sinful people know how to give good gifts to your children, how much more will your heavenly Father give good gifts to those who ask him.
Matthew 7:7-11

What have I asked of others? of God? How can God and others help me on the way to recovery? What can I ask of them?

_____

_____

_____

_____

For Reflection
The Bible says, "God opposes the proud but gives grace to the humble" (James 4:6). How will humility aid me in my recovery? In what ways is pride an obstacle to recovery? In what ways do I display pride and humility in my journey toward recovery?

_____

_____

_____

_____

God blesses those who are poor and realize their need for him, for the Kingdom of Heaven is theirs.
MATTHEW 5:3

Prayer
"Jesus, Son of David, have mercy on me!" (Luke 18:38)

WEEK 8

STEP EIGHT: We made a list of all persons we had harmed and became willing to make amends to them all.

How do I normally find out whom I've wronged? How does the realization that I have wronged someone affect me? Does it affect me differently if the wrongs were intentional as opposed to unintentional?

_____

_____

_____

_____

_____

> If you need ideas, read "Unintentional
> Sins" on page 139 of *The Life Recovery
> Bible.*

Scripture

God in all his fullness was pleased to live in Christ, and through him God reconciled everything to himself. He made peace with everything in heaven and on earth by means of Christ's blood on the cross. This includes you who were once far away from God. You were his enemies, separated from him by your evil thoughts and actions. Yet now he has reconciled you to himself through the death of Christ in his physical body. As a result, he has brought you into his own presence, and you are holy and blameless as you stand before him without a single fault.
COLOSSIANS 1:19-22

When has a broken relationship hindered my relationship with someone else or with God? What was it about that situation that made it difficult for me to relate to others?

_____

_____

_____

_____

For Reflection
To whom can I make amends today? How can I change my behavior to ensure that I don't wrong them this way in the future?

Prayer
God, thank you for forgiving me. Help me as I seek to make amends to those whom I've wronged and to be an agent of your reconciliation. Amen.

WEEK 9

STEP NINE: We made direct amends to such people wherever possible, except when to do so would injure them or others.

How do restitution and reconciliation affect a relationship? How do they affect the community?

_____

_____

_____

Think of a time when someone
sought to make amends to you. How
did you feel? How did you respond?
What was the outcome?

Scripture

Who may worship in your sanctuary, LORD? Who may enter your presence on your holy hill? Those who lead blameless lives and do what is right, speaking the truth from sincere hearts. Those who refuse to gossip or harm their neighbors or speak evil of their friends. Those who . . . keep their promises even when it hurts. . . . Such people will stand firm forever.
PSALM 15:1-5

How does my life measure up to those people described in Psalm 15?
What would my relationships look like if I were more like this?

_____

_____

_____

_____

Try to answer these questions as you
write:

- Do I strive to do what is right?
- Am I consistently honest with others?
  with myself?
- Do I harm those around me, inten-
  tionally or unintentionally, with my
  words?
- Am I willing to make amends to those
  I've wronged, even if doing so may
  hurt me?

For Reflection

How would making this step a habit improve my life? the lives of others?

_____

_____

Prayer

Lord, make me an instrument of Thy peace.
Where there is hatred, let me sow love;
where there is injury, pardon;
where there is doubt, faith;
where there is despair, hope;
where there is darkness, light;
and where there is sadness, joy.

O Divine Master, grant that I may not so much seek
*   to be consoled as to console;*
to be understood, as to understand;
to be loved, as to love;
for it is in giving that we receive;
it is in pardoning that we are pardoned;
and it is in dying that we are born to eternal life. Amen.
—ST. FRANCIS OF ASSISI

WEEK 10

STEP TEN: We continued to take personal inventory, and when we were wrong, promptly admitted it.

Think back over the past few days: What have you done wrong? What have you done right?

_____

_____

_____

_____

Think of your interactions with others in your various contexts—at home, at work, in your community, etc.

Scripture

If my people who are called by my name will humble themselves and pray and seek my face and turn from their wicked ways, I will hear from heaven and will forgive their sins and restore their land.
2 CHRONICLES 7:14

How can I practice the actions listed in this verse (humble myself, pray, seek God's face, turn from my wicked ways) in community with others? Whom can I trust to help me in this? How can I draw strength from and support those people as we seek God together?

_____

_____

Think of those who have been with you in the recovery process. What would work as a support structure for you (e.g., a weekly meeting, a phone call, an e-mail) as you practice this in community with others?

For Reflection

I know that recovery is a process and that there will be successes and failures in the future. How can I respond so that I don't become overconfident because of my successes or depressed because of my failures?

Prayer

God, I'm sorry for _____

_____. Please forgive me, and help me in the future not to make these mistakes again. Help me to humbly accept help and to offer my own strength to others as it's needed. Help me in all things to do what is right, to quickly confess when I'm wrong, and to seek the restoration of my relationships. Amen.

WEEK 11

STEP ELEVEN: We sought through prayer and meditation to improve our conscious contact with God, praying only for knowledge of his will for us and the power to carry it out.

The Bible tells us to pray "at all times and on every occasion" (Ephesians 6:18). What does this mean to you? What would your life look like if you were to pray this way for yourself? for others?

_____

_____

_____

Scripture

When I think of all this, I fall to my knees and pray to the Father, the Creator of everything in heaven and on earth. I pray that from his glorious, unlimited resources he will empower you with inner strength through his Spirit. Then Christ will make his home in your hearts as you trust in him. Your roots will grow down into God's love and keep you strong. And may you have the power to understand, as all God's people should, how wide, how long, how high, and how deep his love is. May you experience the love of Christ, though it is too great to understand fully. Then you will be made complete with all the fullness of life and power that comes from God.
EPHESIANS 3:14-19

How does this description of God and his love make me feel? How would I describe God or his love to someone else?

_____

_____

_____

If you get stuck, write specifically of these attributes listed in the verse:

- Father
- Creator
- generous
- loving
- empowering
- unfathomable

For Reflection

How can I use the resources at my disposal to carry out God's will? As you answer this question, think of these (and other) resources:

- money
- time
- talents
- abilities
- presence

_____

_____

_____

Prayer

All glory to God, who is able, through his mighty power at work within us, to accomplish infinitely more than we might ask or think. Glory to him in the church and in Christ Jesus through all generations forever and ever! Amen. (Ephesians 3:20-21)

WEEK 12

STEP TWELVE: Having had a spiritual awakening as the result of these steps, we tried to carry this message to others, and to practice these principles in all our affairs.

In what areas of my life is it most noticeable that I have begun to practice these principles? In what areas do I still need more work?

Reflect on your contexts (home, work, school, community, etc.), habits, resources (money, time, talents, etc.), and this journal's seasons (heart, soul, mind, and strength) when answering this question.

Scripture

I said, "It's all over! I am doomed, for I am a sinful man. I have filthy lips, and I live among a people with filthy lips. Yet I have seen the King, the LORD of Heaven's Armies." Then one of the seraphim flew to me with a burning coal he had taken from the altar with a pair of tongs. He touched my lips with it and said, "See, this coal has touched your lips. Now your guilt is removed, and your sins are forgiven." Then I heard the Lord asking, "Whom should I send as a messenger to this people? Who will go for us?" I said, "Here I am. Send me."
ISAIAH 6:5-8

Isaiah goes through a process that takes him from being impure, to being purified, to being sent. How can I help others in their recovery, both where I am now and where I envision myself to be in the future?

_____

_____

[God] comforts us in all our troubles so that we can comfort others. When they are troubled, we will be able to give them the same comfort God has given us.
2 CORINTHIANS 1:4

What has my experience taught me about myself? about other people? In what ways can I share these lessons with them?

_____

_____

_____

_____

For Reflection
How did other people help me in my own journey toward recovery? How will their example affect the way I encourage others on the road to recovery?

_____

_____

_____

Think of family, friends, coworkers, or clergy who have worked with you. What characteristics did they display?

_____

_____

Prayer

God, thank you for _____

_____. Please help me to _____

_____. Bring people into my life with whom I can share what you have done for me and whom I can encourage as they seek a deeper relationship with you. Amen.

WEEK 13
Recovering My Life

My Story

What is my story? How has God saved me from myself?

_____

_____

_____

_____

Look over your journal for the Strength season, taking note of the major victories and defeats. Include these in your story. Write your story as you would tell it to someone going through a similar recovery program. What elements of your story would be most beneficial for that person to hear?

My Future

What is my vision for how the community should look and function? How can I use my experience, strength, and resources to benefit the community?

_____

_____

_____

_____

My Plan

What actions can I take to bring about the kind of community I envision? What should my life look like, and what measures can I put into place to ensure I am living this way?

_____

_____

_____

_____

Prayer

Oh, what a miserable person I am! Who will free me from this life that is dominated by sin and death? Thank God! The answer is in Jesus Christ our Lord. . . . So now there is no condemnation for those who belong to Christ Jesus (Romans 7:24–8:1).

INDEX TO THE TWELVE STEPS

FIND HEALING IN GOD'S WORD EVERY DAY.

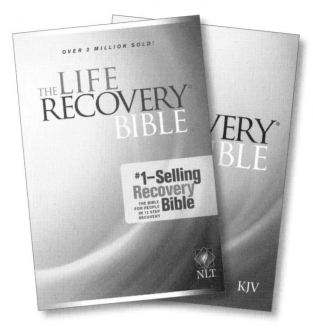

Celebrating over 2 million copies sold!

The Life Recovery Bible is today's bestselling Bible for people in recovery. In the accurate and easy-to-understand New Living Translation, *The Life Recovery Bible* leads people to the true source of healing—God himself. Special features created by two of today's leading recovery experts—David Stoop, Ph.D., and Stephen Arterburn, M.Ed.—include the following:

Recovery Study Notes: Thousands of Recovery-themed notes interspersed throughout the Bible pinpoint passages and thoughts important to recovery.

Twelve Step Devotionals: A reading chain of 84 Bible-based devotionals tied to the Twelve Steps of recovery.

Serenity Prayer Devotionals: Based on the Serenity Prayer, these 29 devotionals are placed next to the verses from which they are drawn.

Recovery Principle Devotionals: Bible-based devotionals, arranged topically, are a guide to key recovery principles.

Find *The Life Recovery Bible* at your local Christian bookstore or wherever books are sold. Learn more at www.LifeRecoveryBible.com.

Available editions:

NLT Hardcover 978-1-4143-0962-0
NLT Softcover 978-1-4143-0961-3
Personal Size Softcover 978-1-4143-1626-0
Large Print Hardcover 978-1-4143-9856-3

Large Print Softcover 978-1-4143-9857-0
KJV Hardcover 978-1-4143-8150-3
KJV Softcover 978-1-4143-8506-8

CP0107

Check out these great resources to help you on your path to recovery:

The Life Recovery Journal has been carefully created to guide you through the recovery process. The questions and quotes will help you to write honest reflections, reinforce what you're learning, and give insight into your recovery as a whole person.

The Life Recovery Workbook is about transformation: from death to life, from addiction to recovery. As you work through each of the Twelve Steps, the challenging spiritual lessons will strengthen you to live free from addiction.

The easy-to-read, down-to-earth meditations in *The Life Recovery Devotional* are designed to help you find the recovery, rest, and peace that Jesus promises. They will help you understand the struggles we all face— in recovery, in overcoming temptation, and in getting back on track after a relapse.